PREFACE

GOING DEEP ON THE WAY

Sitting in church worship services during high school, I found myself re-translating what I heard from the Bible and from the sermon. Why? I really don't know. It just happened. It felt natural. Was this an over-active intuition? Was this the work of the Spirit? This habit, practice, whatever it was, took me deeper into what I was hearing. From those days on, the Word of God was deep and dynamic, intriguing and alive. Beyond high school as I read the Bible more regularly, I would write in the margins of my Bible the questions and insights and re-translations that came to me.

So in the thoughts shared here, I continue to seek to 'go deeper' with what comes to me from words of faith and moments in life. The phrase 'go deeper' implies that the Word of God is much more dynamic and deeper than the particular words both on the page and in human speech. Scripture and church talk get us started on the way to the Word and Truth of God with more listening and insight and understanding to come.

i

This dynamic of going deeper in understanding is, yes, in part intuitive seeing at work and lessons of life learned. Yet it is so much more the larger dynamic of the Spirit's role in leading us deeper into God's Voice to us and God's Truth for us. The set theology teaching of the tradition gets us started on this Way. A much deeper understanding and greater personal transformation await us, wishing to live more fully and deeply into each of us. As we grow more into this dynamic living Word and Truth, our own words and thinking cannot completely capture it...and with the spiritual giants throughout the ages we simply say to it...yes. We sense it more than we know it. We seek to live it, letting God hold the greater knowing.

Going deeper is a call to be vulnerable to how this dynamic and deeper Word and Truth might confront us and shape us and lead us. This going deeper through and beyond theology and faith teachings is our vulnerability and openness to the final mystery that is God and life and truth and faith. This mystery takes us beyond the words and first understandings that the words only begin to carry. We are left in the margins, listening for nudges from the speaking Spirit and the

Notes in the Margin

Bill Calhoun

ISBN 978-1-938859-94-6

Printed by the Tattered Cover Press

www.tatteredcover.com

books@tatteredcover.com

February 2015

greater mystery of Truth. Our words and thoughts point toward this Word and Truth, yet without ever completely knowing the greater Word and Truth that hold us in love and accompany us in life.

I also use the phrase 'go deeper' because of one specific moment in my life. In September of 2000, I asked a person in the congregation to do the Charge to the Installed Minister. Amelie Buchanan charged me to "take us deep" in the faith journey. From that moment, I loved the concept and knew right away that in my previous 28 years of installed ministry, being too busy doing things limited how deep I took myself and the people of the church on the journey of faith. Nine years later when I retired from this last position, I once again had fallen short of "take us deep."

Each of us is invited to go deep in our relationship with God and our engagement with the Word of God. Join me in listening to the nudges, insights, intuitions and deeper meanings of the dynamic Word of God around us, within us and through us. Write in your margins what you hear within yourself. Those inner nudges and insights will take you deeper. They will help take you where you are called to go and towards who you are called to be. In pursuing this "take us deep" path, don't be held back by fear of not getting it right. The traditional box of faith teachings is simply the front door into a deeper and dynamic communion with God. Remember the spiritual giants, after wrestling with Scripture and with life, say that when it comes to ultimate truth, they simply don't know the details....but they do love, trust and walk with God.

Years ago, in reading Psalm 18: 35c, I ran into a problem. The translation said: "Your help (O God) has made me great." Stop the bus, I felt. I did not like the word 'help.' It is too overused....God helps us....which is, yes, true, but too shallow for me...used too easily. At the bottom of the Bible page I found that the Hebrew word can also be translated 'gentleness.' God's gentleness? I love it. Is not the core of our helping others, caring for others, birthed out of a gentleness...on the whole?

And the word 'great.' We live in a world in which being great is worshiped. Our national focus is on those who are 'great.' But in the root meaning of the English word is the concept of rock, granite. So in that first moment, I re-translated the verse: "Your <u>gentleness</u> (O God) has made me a <u>rock</u>." And below in the margin I wrote: And may my gentleness make others a rock.

Go deep!

BE STILL...LET GO

Be still and know that I am God.
                                Psalm 46:10

This is my favorite verse in the Bible. I love to be quiet. I love to 'be still.' Whether sitting outside communing with creation or sitting inside in a 'quiet' chair, to 'be still' is to mentally let go of every task and concern, choosing to be attentive and empty in the fullness of each moment.

In these quiet, reflective moments, I see and clarify how big life is with its mystery and grace. In these quiet, reflective moments, I see and clarify my small part and impact. Yes, we make our best effort at being ourselves and contributing to humankind in love and caring, in helping and serving. Yet, our efforts to contribute to the larger life beyond ourselves begin in this reflective stillness, seeking our right balance and perspective, as we seek to 'see more clearly, love more dearly and follow more nearly, day by day.' (from the musical "*Godspell*" and earlier hymns)

The root Hebrew meaning of this phrase 'be still' is to let your hands fall limp, open, resting....with the message…let go, let go, let go….life is finally out of our hands. These limp, open hands ask us to let go of just about everything…and really everyone. These limp, open hands invite us to rest, letting so much go…and simply be in the moment…present with ourselves and with God. These limp, open, resting hands ask us to be more open to the gifts that God, that life, will give us, more open to the gifts of grace and right paths and open doors that come to each of us….for which we finally can only thank God. The journey with God is first and last our openness to God's Presence with the nudges and guidance and gifts of God's grace, remembering with the spiritual giants that we are 'just passing through.' We let our hands fall limp. These limp hands are serving hands. We live this empty, this simply, this resting quiet. And with these open hands, we are more open to walk hand in hand with each other, getting strength from others, while sharing our strengths with others.

Yes, our hands, hearts and lives do what they can to live well, to be a good neighbor and to make the world a better place. Beyond that, larger hands than ours hold and shape life, as our limp, open, resting hands affirm. This 'be still…let go' insight invites us into the deeper way of faith and new life. This 'be still…let go' insight invites us into a transforming faith and wisdom that fulfills and completes us.

The root understanding of the word 'sacred' is 'to be set apart.' I need to set myself apart for resting, reflection, seeing and deeper understanding. Sitting in my 'quiet' chair, when I truly set myself apart and empty myself into rare moments of non-thinking stillness, I am amazed how the right insight or nudge will suddenly, sacredly, out of supposedly nowhere, come to me and feel like something to which I should pay attention. Many people suggest that we live our lives best and our relationship with God best, in quiet, in silence….as John Phillip Newell suggests… "grounded in God's stillness." (from *Celtic Benediction*)

Psalm 46:10 can rightly be understood as 'be empty [of so much that fills us] and recognize God.' Spiritual giants through time live a certain poverty, which is in part living simply with a certain emptiness of ego and material possessions. This poverty is also about the humility of being empty before, with and in God. Daily, we get to learn how to live this empty, this simply, this resting quiet. I seek more and more to lead with this inner life and trust the right steps in the outer life.

In high school, I came across my dad's ninth grade book of great poetry. The first night that I picked it up, I found Longfellow's poem "The Legend Beautiful." This became one of my favorite poems. The poem wrestles with the tension between serving in the world and hanging out with God. Both are rightly affirmed, summed up with what has been for me a life-guiding line:

"Do your duty, that is best,
Leave unto the Lord the rest."

CHURCH AS CONNECTING

...when you did it to the least of these,
you did it......to me.
Matthew 25:40

When I moved in 2000 to a congregation in Denver, the Word of the Lord came to me boldly through the phone on my desk at church. The phone would ring. Picking up the phone, I would say: "Hello, this is Bill." Huge silence.....then in the silence a click, click, click....and then a recorded voice would laboriously announce... "con-nect-ing." It took me weeks, maybe months, to learn that when the phone rang, I should wait through the silence for the click, click, click, then the laborious voice....."con-nect-ing." This in-my-face nudge got me to thinking about the role of the church as connecting. The church is about connecting with God, connecting with the gathered faith community, connecting with the larger world, and yes, connecting with our selves.

Connecting with God happens as we look to God individually and privately, as well as when we look to God together as a gathered community in worship. We approach this connecting with God through words of

5

scripture, song and prayer, in the hope that these words will lead us and open us to the deeper and greater Presence in us and with us and around us that God is. The true and deeper...."con-nect-ing"....happens beyond the words we speak and hear. Through the mystery of God's Presence and Spirit, a deeper meaning births in us, a connecting we seek to be open to as gift. In the formal worship service, the community together looks God in the eye, seeking this connecting as the community opens up to God's Word and Spirit and Truth. True connecting with God goes on well beyond the sermon and the liturgy through the inner work of each different heart and mind and soul..."con-nect-ing" with God's Presence and new life-giving Word.

One Christmas we shared these words:

In the heart of the Christmas story
God comes to us wrapping our whole being
With light, life, love
Going face to face with us
In one now and forever Embrace
Embracing you, me, all of humankind, all of life
Held as we are in God's
Embrace...life...love...grace...presence
May we embody this Embrace,
Holding each human life in God's safe love.

Connecting with the gathered community that is church is a fascinating mix of human and divine. The church is very human through each needy individual life and personality. Witnessing the church through my lifetime, I see more ego battles and turf tussles than living Jesus, more culture-dominated habits than Word of God-led transformation. Being an institution with rules and practical requirements and need to control, the church faces institutional inertia and bureaucratic bog. Yet the church is more than what happens on Sunday mornings. The Church is what you live each moment, each step, each breath, each person on the daily Way. The true church liturgy is how we live out our lives, living Jesus-love and being open to the daily guidance of the Spirit. The lead piece of living Jesus is about how we connect with each other ….listening, accepting, helping, discerning, loving…in the spirit of Jesus and the Presence of God. Sometimes God's love and spirit lead the church. Sometimes human ego and control lead the church. The difference is dramatic. Yet even as institutional as the church is, the Body of Christ keeps showing up in the shadows, in the engagement of one life with another.

The most important moment in the church's worship service is the moment following the end of the formal worship when people turn to each other to listen, to care, to love… "con-nect-ing."

Connecting with the larger world completes the "con-nect-ing." The church is only completely true church, true Body of Christ, as it moves out of the pews and into the world, "con-nect-ing" as a force of love with each and every person along the way. To meet Christ in the person before you, as the Benedictines and others say, is to truly live Jesus. As each of us leaves the pews to engage in ministry (literally 'waiting upon another'), seeing, listening, caring, loving, we live out Jesus in our loving care and helpful serving….one person at a time, in the quietest, unseen, loving acts of our days. This love of neighbor shapes the common good, the common ground. How often through the years, the teaching of the Gospel turns out to be most transforming when youth move beyond the teachers in their church school classes to mission experiences across the city, the nation and the world.

Out of the pews and the classrooms and into the world, the rubber meets the road, our own eyes are opened, true love is learned, service becomes habit and the 'good news' of the Gospel gets lived out after all. The mission of the church is to live Jesus, each step, each breath, from the smallest acts of kindness to the most dramatic human transformations.

Finally, and first of all, to engage the church, we must get to know our true selves. All this connecting in and through the church is only real as we truly connect with who we are as incomplete and yet blessed human beings. We must connect with ourselves, our struggles, our needs, our fears, before we can hear and honor our inner yearnings to move confidently and lovingly beyond ourselves to God and to others.

As I was graduating from seminary, I asked myself in my journal what I had gotten out of the three years of seminary. What jumped to the top of the list was the sense that God has made us all for life together, that we are in this together.

Life together is the most difficult work that God gives us to do: Click…click…click…"con-nect-ing."

In another Christmas note, we shared these images:

In a child born in the back barn,
God joins the human journey…connecting to care…
One person after another person,
Jesus engages each one…connecting to care…
Our seeing, listening, loving presence
Deepens our…connecting to care….
Christmas marks God's move to us…
connecting to care…
May the best gifts we give be…connecting to care…
As we breathe air in, God breathes into us…
As we breathe out, we breathe into God…
…connecting…to care…
For each other.

FAITH AS TRUST

Trust in the Lord with all your heart
and do not rely on your own understanding.
In all your ways acknowledge God
and God will make straight your paths.
                                    Proverbs 3:5-6

The word faith is built on a core root word meaning 'trust.' Trust is a confidence in and assured reliance and dependence upon another, and religiously, on God.

Sadly, in recent centuries the word faith has been used more as a particular creedal set of beliefs. If you buy into the correct creedal specifics, you have 'faith.' If you don't buy into the exact words and statements, you don't have the right 'faith.' Much religious talk in our time has been tossing out the right phrases to prove our membership in a particular creedal club. Whether in relational or sermon talk, you show your club membership in the words that you use.

Diving into the trust that is faith, we move beyond defining creedal battles to open ourselves to the mystery and vastness which is God before us, around us and within us. In this Presence we grow to trust and

11

love. To live this faith, this trust, we cannot be too busy. The more we live in and through this trust, the more we pace ourselves with a right awareness of life with God and a right awareness of our small but important place in that life with God. We gift our small part, lost, yet found, in God's love and life.

Finding ourselves in this trust mode happens to us more as a gift, a nudge, a calling, that comes at us and to us, rather than as something we initiate. How often a non-church person enters the church in curiosity and leaves captured by something to explore. The faith experience happens to us. In response, we explore this something that chases after our attention. Our exploration usually grows or deepens the trust.

As our faith in the Presence and mystery of God grows or deepens or nudges us, we become a bit less caught up in ourselves and a bit more conscious of and preoccupied with the sense of God with us. We don't get to completely figure out God or life.

Faith in God is finally less proven facts and more a mystery that we go with, that we are open to, that we choose to trust, without fully knowing. As Luke 17:19 puts it:

"your faith [trust] has made you well [whole]....."

I would love to complete my human journey with a more and more complete sense of trust in God. Part of this trust is trust in how my life unfolds, trust in being me, and trust in living out my limits and my dying. This living trust moves in the mystery and vastness that is God with each breath and each step and each moment, here, now, forever.

Some years ago, during a particularly tough day, I noticed the verse on my desk daily Bible verse calendar: *"Though he slay me, yet will I trust in him."* (Job 13:15) To this day, that same calendar page sits open on my desk.

FORGIVEN

Happy are those whose sins are forgiven,
whose sin is covered.
                              Psalm 32:1

Let's get forgiveness straight. Forgiveness is a lead
part of God's love for us. And forgiveness is a lead part
of our love for others. The nature of God's love begins,
leads and ends with forgiveness. God understands and
accepts our humanness as God waits for us to draw
closer to God in oneness.

Now, I know, I know. We sin. Our sin is essentially
living to have life our way over against the in-this-
together of God's way. This orientation 'misses the
mark' (the core meaning of the word sin) that God
creates us to live and be. The church has generally
focused more on our sin than God's forgiving love.
Sadly, this is too often as a way to control us. This
focus on human sin sets God apart and above us when
the God that I know wants daily to walk with us and
talk with us and enjoy our very human journey with us

15

until this companionship transforms us into a new and more faithful life and a deeper love.

This God-move-to-us invites us to stop, look and listen to its meaning. From the beginning, "God so loved the world." In that love, God covers our sin. God comes to humankind to share our death and our ego battles and our humanness. In Jesus Christ, God comes to make this love clear and close, seeking to hang out with us in companionship and communion through this bumpy human journey until we finally understand what our new and selfless life in and with God is all about. When we finally arrive at this truth, we return the embrace of God's forgiving love. Our behaviors, life choices and spirits express this embrace. Once we open our eyes to this life and love coming at us and for us, our 'new' life work is to move from ourselves to God, from me to we, from ego to soul.

Our response to this love is the core meaning of the word REPENT….to go, to act, in a new and better way, closer 'to the mark,' to the life which we are called to live and be. We are happy because God loves us. We are happy to live in and through God, each breath, each step, each moment, together. We are happy, because

God's love understands us and forgives us. This love holds us, awaiting our move beyond ourselves. Our move to God and to our fellow humans begins and completes itself in God's love.

God's forgiveness is like a hiding place for me, as Psalm 32:7 says: *"You are a hiding place for me."* I love this line. I am reminded of my several secret forts as I was growing up….a tree in Atlanta….a water cooler tower in Houston…my bedroom in Detroit…my rock in Colorado. God's Presence is like hiding out in a secret fort. God's Presence takes us away from the daily life of the world, 'in the world but not of the world.' Hiding out with God, we seek to be open to the truth of these words: *"I will instruct you and teach you the way you should go; I will counsel you with my eye upon you."* (Psalm 32:8) This *"eye"* upon us is no prison guard or demanding priest but the gaze of God's love. *"Instruct you"*…..the inward sense of being called to the right path….the Jesus path….the love path. It is the nature of the heart of God to hold us in safe love, which forgives as it draws us closer into a real and living 'oneness.' The focus is on us, not in a punishing mode, but rather in an opportunity mode to realign, to grow closer, to walk together, talk together and be One.

May we walk the earth happy, open to this forgiveness as we fumble and bumble through our egos and fragility and wrong decisions. May we let this sense of forgiveness set us free to live more and more in the right paths of love and life....forgiven on our way to our completion in God.

FREEDOM

It was for freedom that Christ set us free.
Galatians 5:1

Throughout the unfolding history of democratic societies, humankind holds a creative tension between individual freedom and the in-this-together community common good. Both are critical truths to be upheld in a healthy democratic society. This was the main dance for the American Founding Fathers. This same dance continues today between 'me' and 'we,' between individual freedom, so very important, and a common good that helps grow greater freedom for each person and for all. In our time, the "me the people" passion of what I want to defend for myself is as strong as ever, built on 'me,' my ego and 'my freedom.' The case for the freedom of the common good choice requires going deeper to find.

While offering opening prayers in the Colorado State Senate, I found that one political party began the opening daily ceremony with the Pledge to Allegiance to the flag, and then the opening prayer followed.

When the other political party was in the majority, the opening ceremony began with an opening prayer followed by the Pledge of Allegiance to the flag. Do we lead by looking to the country or looking to God? The dance goes on.

One of the most common lines in the church is "we have always done it this way." The implication is that we want our freedom to do church the way we always have done church. Don't ask us to change. This gets to the biggest problem with Jesus, who was always asking folks to go with him in a new way. As we begin to move from reflecting on ourselves to reflecting on a relationship with and in God, in Jesus, in the Spirit, what does this shift from 'me' to 'we' say about freedom?

Karl Barth suggests that God is the only one who is truly free. The rest of us find ourselves in human community caught in the dance between ourselves and relationships with others, between what we want and what is good for us together.

And in God's freedom, God longs for each of us to be free. This freedom is in Christ. As we live in this Way, our true freedom is in and of God and in loving service to God, ourselves and each other. We are set free for a new way of being. Barth suggests that in God, we become rich, while we ourselves meet a certain poverty of self in this larger relationship. In Christ we are set free from 'me' for so much more.

Yes, we are free…free to choose this path, this relationship. But we are not completely and truly free ourselves because we find ourselves committed to a greater love than for ourselves…a love for God and a love for neighbor which restricts the 'me' freedom.

Free? Yes and no. The sense of freedom feels good. The sense of commitment beyond the purely 'me' freedom feels even better.

GOD OUR COMPLETION

God is our refuge and our strength,
a very present/well proven help.
                                    Psalm 46:1

We wear out…but always into God…our completion.
From our birth through our days and years of
humanness and on into our death, we meet our human
limits of insights and energy and control of life. What
lies beyond these limits is the Presence of God whose
life, spirit and being complete us. This completion is
not just in death, but from birth on, for death and birth
are together as one shared story. As we eventually wear
out physically, we wear out into a larger reality of
God's grace, love, light and life. Richard Rohr
describes it as 'falling upwards into God.' In this
completion, we humans arrive where we are made and
meant to be and know and live.

When we focus on ourselves, our lives are less than this
completion. Yes, we must work for food, clothing,
shelter and the common good. But do we do this on our

own or in and with God? When we only focus on our minor part in the greater whole, the One who is the source and completeness of life is missing or less central. Yet, in and with God, mystery that God is, we find an all-consuming and life-giving companion. The more we live into God, the more we are filled with God rather than with ourselves.

God humbly enters our humanness to meet us and guide us to a deeper dimension of life beyond ourselves. God holds our human fumbling and bumbling with love. In this relationship, we find ourselves complete...not perfect...still human...yet spiritually held and whole. Do we understand completely and exactly this completion? No. Can we be open to this promise of completion? Yes, in the trust that is our faith.

Our way to this completion finds help in Biblical teachings, practices and rules, which help shape our thinking and focus our orientation. These rules are less about church-controlled obedience and more coaching points that help us move closer to God in life and love. God is not a puppeteer who controls our lives but rather a companion who walks with us, talks with us, guides us and seeks to transform our lives into the completion that we meet and enjoy in God. This Presence of God clarifies the right balance of our lives. This completion is God's companionship with us. We meet this companionship as we get to know the grace flow that lives and flows in, through and around us in God's living Presence. We meet this companioning completion in God's love, which is greater than the limits of our human love. We meet this completion in the speechless awe of creation's beauty and wonder. We meet this completion in the center of our souls.

Hebrew words frequently describe the nature of this companion: *"God is merciful and gracious, slow to anger, and abounding in steadfast love." (Psalm103:8)* In this companionship and Presence, God sticks with us (which is the implication of "steadfast love") and is patient with us in accompanying us. God's companionship affirms that God is with us…in our face… choosing to walk with us and talk with us and call us God's own. The companionship of God is not possessive or controlling. God walks with us and completes us in the way of relationship, friendship, companionship, love.

On my own I come up short of the mark. In God I can be myself and yet find my deepest self and my completion. Our true penitence is our awareness of our misalignment with God. Our true obedience is our effort at alignment and realignment through seeking more specifically and intentionally in each breath and step and moment to live Jesus, to walk the Way, to be open to the Spirit. This completion becomes our true value, our true wealth, our true being.

Happy is the one who listens to me,
watching daily at my gates,
waiting beside my doors.
For whoever finds me/God finds life.
Proverbs 8: 34-35

GOD'S SAFE LOVE

We know we have passed from death into life
when we have loved one another.
                                        1John 3:14

This sense of God's safe love first came to me in a
worship service. Standing on the chancel steps, I had
just led the congregation in the Unison Prayer of
Confession. Out of the silence following that prayer,
my role was to remind us all of God's forgiveness,
which in that congregation we called the Assurance of
God's Love. At that point in the service, the church
choir stood in the middle of the aisle of the big neo-
Gothic sanctuary. The choir that morning was the
Denver Gay Men's Chorus. Before me stood 75 gay
men who fully knew that their sexual orientation was
not safe in the larger church, including in the
congregation in which they were presently standing. In
that moment, the thought came to me that these men are
not safe with us, the church, but thank God, they are
safe with God. And I said this: we are usually not safe
with each other, but in the God that we know in Jesus

27

Christ, we are safe to be ourselves, safe with God, safe in God's love.

Yes, the lead piece of the Christian belief in being right with God is by us "behaving" according to the rules and laws of the Bible and the church. Our misbehaving is our sin, in which we 'miss the mark' that God's life and love call us to live out. In this human predicament, the church lays out that our only right path to God is in accepting Christ as our Savior through whom a right relationship with God is earned for us.

Yet, as I go deeper in my experience of God, I find from scripture that God leads with love, a patient love. God creates each and every one of us in love, comes to us in love through Jesus, engages us in love and holds out for us in love. To say yes to Jesus is to say yes to the love with which God holds us from beginning to end, companions us in our diverse humanness and through our death. In other words, in this love that is God, we have been and always will be 'safe.'

God's safe love holds us from our beginning, just as we are, as diverse as we are. God's safe love waits for each of us to learn to accept and love ourselves and to learn to accept and love our diverse fellow human beings. In Jesus Christ we are called to keep each one before us, ourselves and others, safe in God's love. Little practices help with this, like finding a piece of ourselves in the one before us, as different as that one is, acknowledging their struggles and our own struggles, remembering that God made us in all our diversity for life together in a safe and welcoming love. In God's safe love, we can live this out.

In the spirit of God's safe love, these are new words to sing with the hymn "*Just as I am.*"

> *Just as I am, myself, these days,*
> *Created by God to live God's praise.*
> *And to my life, God says to me,*
> *Come closer, mine, come close to me.*
>
> *Just as we are, ourselves to be,*
> *Diversity makes humanity.*
> *And to my neighbor, unlike me,*
> *Come closer, friend, come close to me.*

GOD'S WORLD

This is my Father's world, and to my listening ears
All nature sings, and round me rings
The music of the spheres.
This is my Father's world: I rest me in the thought
Of rocks and trees, of skies and seas;
His hand the wonders wrought.
                    Hymn: This is My Father's World

The van I was driving was full of young people heading out of town on a mission work trip. As we headed to Interstate 80, a voice from the back of the van yelled out: "There's Wally's World!" We were driving by the new Walmart store that had just opened. Its presence was already closing down local businesses in our 15,000 person Iowa town as the former culture of small, local businesses gave way to large, global business with new dynamics that move beyond the workers to the profits.

Hearing "Wally's World" led my mind directly to the concept of God's World. Before we were on the interstate, the contrasting images of Wally's World and God's World, of the world of human practices and the world of God's practices, surged through my mind.

I had never liked the word 'kingdom,' as in the Kingdom of God. Why? Kings are men in a world God created with women and men. The concept of kingdom suggests a non-elected, often controlling human ruler. From that moment on, I have preferred to refer to God's World rather than the Kingdom of God.

For us, God's World is a new way and order of living our lives, a resetting of the human way with new and different values. In God's World, our human condition and interactions are inspired by and centered in God's move to us in Jesus Christ. In God's World, we are called to share our human life together through enjoying and loving God, enjoying and loving our neighbors, and yes, enjoying and loving our own personal life journeys. In God's World we stay focused and open with God. Committed to God's World, we get up every morning and live where we are and what we do as citizens of God's World. We grow into our new life, our rebirth, in the simplest moments and in the major transformations, to be the people that God births us to be.

And what does this have to do with heaven? Everything. Jesus made clear that heaven is here and now, so God's World is our world now and forever. As we grow spiritually, we move from ego to soul, moving in effect from our world to God's World. And what is the instructional manual for this new world? Live as Jesus lives.

And in the spirit of God's World, these words sung by the Taize Community:

All along my way, you've been with me.
Even now, O Lord, Your Spirit goes before me.

GRACE FLOW

For by grace you have been saved through faith,
and this is not your own doing;
it is the gift of God – not the result of works,
so that no one may boast.
Ephesians 2: 8-9

Set your hope fully on the grace to be given you.
I Peter 1:13

In New York City, I lived across Broadway Avenue from the seminary. Daily crossing Broadway, I noticed an interesting dynamic. Some days when I came down the front building steps to the sidewalk and turned right for the ten steps to the light for crossing Broadway, the light would turn red. I stopped and waited. On other days, down the steps, turning right, as I approached the light at Broadway, the light would turn green. What caught my attention was that on the days that the light turned green, many events and thoughts and conversations really clicked. I began calling those moments 'green light moments.' On days the light turned red, it seemed there were less green light moments through the day.

35

That crossing light led me to pay more attention to how things in my days, conversations, insights, and events, came together as green lights or red lights. I began to call these green light moments the flow of God's grace. And over the past twenty-five years or so, in my morning quiet time, I affirm my eagerness to watch through the day for how the right pieces come together for good in God's World. I seek to stay open to these green lights, this grace flow, in which 'right' and helpful insights, 'promptings' and happenings occur.

I have no interest in writing a profound and accurate theological analysis of this flow of God's grace. In and with God, the grace flow has always been there and will always be there. I simply want to continue to watch the flow of God's grace through, around and in my life and in the lives around me. Yes, I understand that in the core Christian teaching, it is God's grace that saves us. And I am saying 'yes' to that. Yet most people stop there and say, ok, thanks. But the core of the word salvation is centered on wellness [being in a healthy and right spot] and on deliverance [finding the right path]. Deliverance is the central dynamic of the grace flow which leads us in the right paths and, in effect, to our 'salvation' in the best sense. Or as Karl Barth writes: *God's grace tends to make good what we humankind tend too often to do badly.*

My experience of God's grace is that it is a life force that leads, shapes and sustains God's World, now and forever. The grace flow is standard operating procedure. The grace flow is God's faithfulness in our face. Like the steady flow of blood, of oxygen, there is a steady flow of grace, of paths of grace, of life moments to be fed by and to build upon. The right agenda, the right path, shows up for us through this flow of God's grace. So when Andrew Young writes: *"Coincidence is God's way of being anonymous,"* I say yes!

Our challenge is to live and breathe our openness and awareness to this central reality in and through our lives. Is the grace flow something we have to earn? No, the grace flow is part of the gift of the love and caring and leading that is God's World. So what do we do to be open to it? It helps if we are walking humbly with God, living loving kindness and communing with creation and humankind in speechless awe.

The common spiritual/faith word 'surrender' is the simple yet wise yielding to, rather than opposing, the flow of life, which at its core is the grace flow.

In the resurrection accounts, the disciples, thinking the dead Jesus has left them behind, instead get the word that *'he is going ahead of you.'* I love this phrase. A devotional years ago suggested that each time I walk down a hospital hallway to visit someone, I remember that *'he is going ahead of you.'* In that spirit, may we be open to the mysterious Presence of the flow of God's grace, the working of the Spirit, the resurrected Christ...going before us.

> *Amazing Grace, how deep the joy,*
> *That guides a life like me.*
> *I make my way as best I can,*
> *Until I truly see.*

GRATITUDE

...make thanksgiving your sacrifice to God...
Psalm 50:14

Anne Lamott has long said that if we can only say one
word to God, that word is 'thanks.'

Sister Mary Dingman, my long time spiritual director,
encouraged me to make a gratitude list daily. "What do
you do when your head hits the pillow at night?" she
asked. She encouraged me to review the day and,
mentally or in a journal, list the moments in my day for
which I was most grateful. Through the years those
moments have covered anything from a look in an eye
or a stirring of leaves to a time with another person or a
resolution of an important event. These paths of grace
lead to grounds of gratitude. This practice of reviewing
gratitude moments leads to gratitude being more
conscious 24/7.

More and more, I find myself seeking to over thank others through my days, and of course, to constantly thank God for the green lights of our days and for the beauty of the earth and life and love.

Thanks is what sacrifice in the Bible is really about. It begins with killing an animal or taking some of one's possessions off the top (cattle, sheep, crops, money) and sharing what we have with God. We sacrifice what we have not to earn something but to simply say thanks.

In the root word of sacrifice is the core word 'sacred.' Sacred is that which is 'set apart.' And the more you and I are filled with gratitude, even in our hardest times, the more we 'set apart' our spirits and our lives in the sacredness of gratitude.

HANGING OUT WITH GOD

I will bless the Lord at all times...
God's praise shall continually be in my mouth...
Happy are those who take refuge in God...
Those who seek the Lord lack no good thing.
The Lord is near....
From Psalm 34

It has taken me a lifetime to move from the now and then prayers to God that I 'should' and want to do to the radical move of hanging out with God 24/7. How do I do this hanging out with God?

It is both an ongoing learning experience and a growing practice. When I stop at a red light, I seek to pay attention to my breathing and to watch the faces of fellow human beings who walk or drive by. I notice the clouds, the trees and the birds. This exercise helps me get to the present moment in hopes of releasing my mind from the to-do lists and concerns. With my breathing and my seeing, I remember my communion with creation, my caring for others and the Presence of God.

Early on in my faith journey, the lead piece seemed to be to say to others the right things about God. Now, I say less and less to others about God. More and more, I enjoy sensing God's Presence, feeling fully embraced by God in each moment, each breath, each step. This speechless sense of Presence may help us make the greater witness to God in how we live, how we respond, how we are present in each moment.

Yes, there are specific prayers to pray as I go to sleep and as I wake up. But even my prayer life has become less traditional prayers and more simply being quiet in the Presence of God, sensing God's Presence with those I think about and pray for. In this awareness, in this attentiveness, in this sense of God's Presence, I try to let go of the past and let go of the future and simply be with God in that moment. In this Presence, I seek to trust God's companionship and strength as life unfolds. In this trust, I seek to let go of worry and of what to do and say. As I hang out with God, I will find my way.

I would like to get to the point that I do this really well….even through conversations and work projects….each breath and each step and each moment….sensing and enjoying the Presence of God. Push my shoulders back. Be conscious of my breathing fully, deeply. Living in God's love, here, now, deep and light.

Is that all? To start with and end with….yes!

LETTING GO INTO DEATH

If we live, we live to the Lord.
And if we die, we die to the Lord;
So then, whether we live or whether we die,
we are the Lord's.
Romans 14: 8-9

People who are dying share clues about what lies beyond our physical death. I remember a Sunday afternoon in a nursing home, sitting quietly by the bedside of a dying woman. She had been in a coma for some time, restless and breathing with difficulty. Suddenly her countenance became relaxed and a light gently glowed from her face. Then, quietly, she stopped breathing. The light that emerged on her face was a clue to the light ahead, which appears to so many people who go through near death moments. This light affirms that we are a people of change, on our way to God, who does not change. We die on the way to our new creation.

In the hours and days before their physical bodies die, many people relate having visitations from friends and loved ones. When I saw a long time older friend who was waiting to die in the hospital, he asked me lucidly about our kids, following my responses clearly and with interest. Then suddenly he said: "Oh, there is my friend the judge [his best friend] and oh, there's my wife." He pointed toward the empty chairs at the end of his bed. The judge and his wife had died years before.

As my mother was waiting to die, she would jokingly speak of waiting for a helicopter to come and pick her up. Several others have used the image of waiting for their train to depart. Mom would also laugh about how she was soon to turn into a butterfly as she moved on beyond death. To this day, when I see a butterfly, I often say or think, "Hi, Mom."

Sitting with my mom in her last days, as she went in and out of sleep, I noticed her eyes moving back and forth. "What are you seeing? I asked. "Some women with children," she said. "Why don't you talk with them, Mom?" I suggested. Our shared silence in her sleepiness continued. About twenty minutes later, she said, "They want me to come with them." An evening later, an aide came in to turn Mom. As she was turned, Mom said to someone not visible in the room, "But I don't know how to come with you." She died the next evening.

Occasionally, new widows will share that they had a dream about a visit from their recently deceased spouse. On one occasion as I met with a new widow to plan her husband's funeral service, she told me that that morning, she had had a dream in which several of her relatives who had died came to her asking her to let them plan the funeral service.

Another dynamic of having one foot in this world and one in the next involves the need to finish a relationship before one lets go into death and beyond. The nurse in the hospital could not believe that with his vital signs as weak as they were, Roger Wheeland was still alive. His son Charlie was driving to see him from 90 miles away. Within twenty minutes of Charlie's arrival, Roger let go and died.

Others die before their vital signs would suggest so. In two different situations, I was sitting near a person in bed and their family member by their side. In one situation, the son kept insisting that his mother be fed when she did not want to eat because she was ready to die.

In the conversation before me, the mother finally assured her son that it was ok to let her die. We continued to talk, and I fed her ice chips. Thirteen minutes after they had settled the issue with tears and love, Erma suddenly died.

Another time, sitting with Frank and his dying sister, I asked them what they loved about each other. The sister in bed spoke first with humor and honesty. Then Frank looked his sister in the eye and told her his feelings about her. He looked back at me when he completed his thoughts. We turned back to the sister. She had died.

I have suggested to folks before surgery, and also as they wait to die, to picture themselves floating on a comfortable rubber raft in an ocean. Relax on that raft, I encourage them. The raft will hold you up, safely. The ocean is God's love, which will always hold you up, close and safe.

Relax into surgery. Relax into dying. Relax into God's love and life which are with you now and forever. As our body wears out, we let go into the larger reality of the Spirit and a larger Life.

LIVE JESUS

By this we may be sure that we are in him:
Whoever says 'I live in him,'
Ought to walk just as he walked.
                                    I John 2: 6

Reading about Jesus, it comes to me that I am called to live Jesus…not to be Jesus…but to live Jesus. What does this mean? To live Jesus means to try to live the way Jesus invites us to live. Living Jesus lives out our faith.

Yes, we are more human than divine. Yes, we fumble and bumble our caring for others [as well as our caring for ourselves]. And yes, the coaching points of Jesus are the goals we seek to meet, the love we seek to share, and the pathway we seek to walk. Quiet reflective time at the beginning of the day and reflective check-in moments at stop lights and other reflective moments during the day help keep us focused on these goals, this love, this 'Way' [as the early church was known].

To live Jesus is to lead with the inner life and trust the right steps in the outer life. We lead with a life of prayer where prayer is a 24/7 attention to and awareness of God's Presence and love holding us and holding others. In hanging out with God in this Way, we seek to shift from our ego-led responses to a greater openness beyond our ego and beyond our self. This daily attempt to live differently, to be changed, to be a new self, is the heart of growing into a living companionship with this One who loves to accompany us on this interesting human journey.

To live Jesus, we speak less and listen more. In the Gospels, Jesus engages others with questions and then listens to their lives. This engagement brings people alive and, through listening, opens the Way for love to be received and channeled. This listening, in the spirit of Francis of Assisi, is listening to the bird song, the ocean waves, children's voices, stirrings of the wind, and the deeper and broader speechless silence that holds all life together. This listening is a stillness of seeing, a calmness of hearing.

To live Jesus is to move from professing our faith to living our faith. For example, take the cross of our faith. In and through the cross, Jesus makes space for God by trusting and loving God through laying down his own life. And in the cross, Jesus makes space for us by sharing our life and our death. In this spirit, the cross speaks of God's determination in Jesus to stick with us. And in the cross, we find our determination to stick with each other.

To live Jesus, we must get out of the pew and live our faith in the world. We begin as we turn to each other leaving the pews and listen to the human heart before us, greeting the Christ in each person. To live Jesus continues as our loving, listening presence strengthens family life and friendships. As my father moved from the pews into the world, he would always say: 'you go first' and 'here, let me help you.' In the spirit of the sacrament of communion, we, in and with Jesus, are broken open for others, giving our lives to care for others. This 'healing hospitality' is the nature of God's embrace of love for us and for all humankind. Our presence in our days is to be this 'healing hospitality.'

To live Jesus is to remember that "*the government is upon his shoulders.*" Before God we get only a little piece of life, of relationships, of power, of understanding. We trust this little bit with gratitude and do our small part with joy.

To live Jesus, we walk the earth more and more aware of the human injustices right before us and around us and consider how we might address them in our small way. In the face of racism, each soul we face we hold and honor in God's safe love. In the face of war and violence, we hold each life before us, safely and in God's peace. As we leave the pew, we find our own ways to help and to care, to be fair, just, right. In a lifetime, our gifting of caring and serving is quite small, and preferably unseen. Our gifting is our drop into the ocean of God's love and caring.

To live Jesus raises the dead in the sense of bringing people alive in a new way....feeding the hungry, walking with the least among us, engaging in programs that reach out to others. I think we need to take Jesus to people less and live Jesus with people more. To begin with, we engage others in a way that brings them alive through smile, hope, energy, peace, confidence. In this mode we live humbly, love completely, do justice.

To live Jesus is to live simply, consume simply, schedule simply, speak simply. Less is more. Meister Eckhard puts it this way: "The spiritual life has much more to do with subtraction than it does with addition."

And Richard Rohr: "All great spirituality is about letting go." Living Jesus is less about addition and more about subtraction, less about consuming and more about sharing.

Living Jesus we find the grace of caring for the 'least' among us. We choose selflessness and caring over selfishness and consumption. We are called to live this loving presence and nothing more. Living Jesus is traveling light. We live simply that our own transformation may gift others.

To live Jesus, we seek to let the Christ Spirit and God's love flow in and through us. We seek to line up with this Spirit and love and channel it through us. And to do this, we become less visible to ourselves and to others.

As I have read in my favorite devotional book, Letters from the Scattered Brotherhood:

> *Keep invisible in the visible world...*
> *Immortal in a mortal world...*
> *Eternal in a changing world...*
> *Continually reborn in a dying world.*

LIVING THE WAY

I am the way, the truth and the life.
John 14:6

...loving the Lord your God, walking in all God's ways,
and holding fast to God...
Deuteronomy 11:22

The early followers of Jesus were known as, and called, 'the Way.' The core meaning of Jesus' word 'repent' was this: I invite you to come with me in a 'new way, a new direction.' In that spirit, Jesus speaks of new or fresh wineskins. Knowing the habits of the human heart, Jesus calls us to a new way of being, an openness that reshapes and re-aligns us in relationship with God, with ourselves and with each other.

Jesus calls us to live for others as we live in and with and, yes, for God. 'Come follow me' is about a Way that is new to us, that is beyond 'me' on the way to 'us.' The Way is a new and deeper human life to live. As God is for us, 'right' with us, and righteous towards us, we are moved to live in this new way to be for, to live for, one another.

55

This new Way is before us to follow as it unfolds in 'right paths.' The longer I live, the more intrigued I am by the intuitive promptings within me. Of course, we must examine and evaluate and discern our promptings and nudges that come from within. The more we do, the more we recognize the promptings that are from God, of the Spirit, of Jesus, that come to us from within us and yet beyond us. Our lives are inspired to move from our own wants to God's ways. And God's grace moves, love and companionship humble and inspire our own efforts and moves.

Only as the followers of Jesus became more organized, and through the organizing became more divided, taking sides and positions, did the church become the complex, diverse and divisive institutional battle ground that it is today, moving from walking 'the Way' to following the 'church.' By now the followers of Jesus have become so overwhelmed by the 'church' that the institutional way too often distracts us from the original Way of the followers of Jesus.

Living the Way is a life of walking together. This ministry of walking catches the spirit of the road to Emmaus story (Luke 24), when two are walking and talking, listening and sharing together, and the Risen Christ shows up.

May you and I find our right paths to walk together and follow 'the Way.' This Way invites us to the Jesus move of walking with others, listening to others, caring for others. And this kind of living and loving is at best an unseen loving presence.

In most faith communities, I see 'the Way' in action. As formal worship concludes, small groups huddle to check in and care for each other, to follow up with each other, to walk with each other. This checking in leads small groups to give themselves to food pantries and student mentoring and Bible studies and hospital visits and on to medical and service mission trips across the city, the nation and the world.

It all begins with one person choosing to walk with another person, listening, caring, helping, companioning….the ministry of walking together. And in the conversations along the Way, in the spirit of the Emmaus Road story, God shows up, love shows up, faith is birthed, and life together comes alive.

LIVING INTO THE LIGHT

And God said. 'Let there be light.' And there was light.
Genesis 1:3

And the city has no need for sun or moon to shine on it,
for the glory of God is its light.
Revelation 21:23

These verses come from the beginning and the end of
the Hebrew Christian scriptures. Creation begins with
the gifting of light into the dark nothingness that was
'in the beginning.' In the Book of Revelation, our life
journey heads toward and finally arrives in the city of
God, where God is fully present. God's Presence fills
the city with light. In the Creation that you and I know
as life, light is the beginning and the end, our guide and
companion. In the midst of our human journey with its
darkness, anxiety and lostness, our task and our
opportunity is to live into this light that is our beginning
and, throughout life, our true home.

Over the past thirty-five years, I have had two
formative dreams in which light jumped out at me to
catch my attention. I began doing dream work with
Morton Kelsey in the fall of 1977. I would place a

notebook by my bed for writing down my dream notes right after the dream happened. Through the years since, I continue to journal my significant dreams.

Two or three years after beginning this dream work, I had the following dream: I bought a New York Times newspaper and boarded a train. As I read the paper, the train went through a long, dark tunnel. I noticed the great darkness and gave thought to being in a tunnel deep in the earth. After a while the train arrived at the edge of a Swiss-like mountain. I began to walk up toward the top of the mountain through a pasture with gentle brooks weaving their way through the grass and flowers of this green pasture. As I approached the top of the mountain, I realized that there was nothing beyond the top. And at the top, I looked down into what I knew instantly was the famous abyss of life.....the deep darkness of nothingness. I was fascinated rather than worried or scared, intrigued to see for myself the abyss of life, the dark pit of nothingness. I stood there quietly, looking into the darkness. Eventually, I sensed a bit of light in the darkness.

As I focused on this slight light, the light became more visible. In this growing light amidst the vast darkness, I began to see a small path going down into the abyss. As the light became clearer, I walked down the path, slowly, carefully. Before long, I realized that the light was coming from a cave in the side of the mountain. Finally I stood before the cave and could see an altar table. The light was coming from behind the altar. In the quiet, suddenly, I heard these words: "God is One."

In another dream, more recently, I was getting a room organized, relieved to be completing the ordering. As I was finishing up, I noticed a large wax candle with its burning wick clearly calling my attention. As the dream was ending, I looked at the wax of the candle, melting as it does. The thought came to me: 'as I wear down, I share a light that is not my own.'

These dreams continue to hold my attention. Light is the lead piece in the dreams. On our human journey, light keeps catching our attention, from dawn to dusk, from stars to Hanukkah to prayer candles to night lights.

One winter morning, flying from Denver to Kansas City for my annual monastery retreat, I was seated by the right window. As the plane took off heading east, I watched the orange ball of the sun rise out of the eastern Colorado earth, slowly, holy, awe-filled. That afternoon, as Jim Gordon and I walked outside to the nearby chapel for evening prayers, I looked to the west and watched the same orange ball of the sun slipping into the Kansas earth, slowly, holy, awe-filled. The mystery and majesty of the sun catching my attention that day still deeply moves me.

In recent years, my prayer life has grown more into a contemplative quiet of watching the play of light. As the light plays on high mountain peaks or on a hanging ivy plant or on human faces, I see God's light shining on us and in us. May the lives that we live reflect this light. And may we honor and reflect the light that we see shining in others.

> *"The Lord is my light..."*
> *Psalm 27: 1*

MEETING GOD IN CREATION

For the beauty of the earth, for the glory of the skies,
For the love which from our birth,
Over and around us lies.
Lord of all, to you we raise,
This our song of grateful praise.
Hymn: For the Beauty of the Earth

Looking back over my human journey, communion with creation is for me a lead piece of God and of hanging out with God in my life. It began in my earliest years by leaving the house and sitting on a rock or in a tree or by a stream, sitting in speechless awe, noticing and engaging life and beauty. Through the years, I grew to pay more and more attention to the play of light on leaves and faces. I love to note the spirit of leaves reaching out to me, dancing in the breeze, offering fragrance and shading privacy. The variety of flowers, weeds and plants welcome me into the complexity, variety and expanse of creation. And I love to stand before the breaking waves of the ocean that say to me…release…let go…fall into being.

The lead path into creation is in walking. The longer we walk, the more we let go of things on our minds and give more and more attention to the beauty of the earth, the glory of the skies.

The sky moves me from attention to small details to speechless awe over the vast reaches of time and space. The play of light at sunrise and sunset speaks of holiness. The stars in the vast sky speak of wonder and mystery. Even surging storms teach how small our human storms really are. And undergirding all this attention to creation is attention to the Creator God who has added us to the leaves and to the stars. This attention to creation reminds us of how vast God and life are, inviting us to acknowledge and find our own small place and live our given day gratefully, faithfully and simply...thinning into God.

In more recent years, I have been led to Celtic Christianity, which has always included attention to God's creation as part of the journey with God. This creation-centered focus disturbed the controlling church through the ages and still does not fit in well with traditional theology.

But for a kid who liked to sit on rocks and observe, and to a man who loves to sit out on the deck and breathe in the sky and the stars, Celtic Christianity is an affirming guide and help.

More and more of us walk in the park for exercise with our eyes on our phones, checking calendars and texts. I hope that those folks will occasionally look up and catch a glimpse of God's Presence and love in the multi-dimensions of the creation around us. Light plays on leaves and from human eyes. Wind moves around us from gentle to strong, suggestive of the Spirit's moves in and around us. Mountains and seas, trees and flowers, invite each of us into a larger world of beauty and togetherness. And the vast sky of stars and space leaves us in speechless awe. In these moments, God is in us, and we are in God.

PRAYER

Only the one who seeks everything in God
prays to God.
And yet again only the one who seeks nothing in oneself
seeks everything in God.
                              Karl Barth

In my early years in the church, formal church prayer was taught as five basic and regular types, expressed through the various parts of the formal worship service: Praise; Confession of Sin; Intercession; Petition; Thanksgiving. The church also taught me that there is the prayer of small groups for healing, listening, discerning. Finally, there are the personal prayers of each individual.

This is a fair structure and guide. Yet this prayer does not go deep enough for me. Growing to love the Psalms, I understood that many of the Psalms were birthed out of the solitude of the psalmist hanging out with God, asking questions, sharing anger and doubt, going on and on until…aha…a thought from God would come out of the silence. This quiet listening conversation with God and the psalmist seems to be the core dynamic of prayer.

On the way to having God speak to me in prayer, reading Dietrich Bonhoeffer encouraged me to begin prayer with a phrase of scripture and let that Word from God shape and work on the prayer conversation with God. For years, my starting Word in a time of prayer would be scripture, usually the Psalms, and also reading from a 'devotional' book. In the context of that listening conversation together, I would run through my prayer list of persons and events.

In seeking to go deeper in prayer, I tried to meditate. I won and lost with my meditation effort. I could not find the technique and right mantra that worked for me. So I finally just sat in quiet...until I reached complete, empty quiet...complete, empty silence...including sometimes almost falling asleep...that quiet. And then, like the Psalmist, insights, nudges and inner promptings would well up like a underground spring. When I asked John Phillip Newell how I might go deeper in prayer, he encouraged me to pay attention to my 'yearnings.' Perhaps the Psalmist says yes to this in Psalm 16:7:

"...my heart instructs me."

More and more, prayer for me is just being silent. In later years, I have sat in the morning quiet and thoughtlessly watched sunlight come through a window and play upon a hanging ivy plant. I gave myself to the focused task of awe that I found in the play of the light. And out of my willingness to be silent, prayer became more and more a hanging out with God, awake to and cherishing the sense of God's Presence, of God's Love, just being together. In and through this silence together, I found in this fellowship, in this communion, the strength and Presence of God's companionship in my life and the life around me. Starting the day in this deep, quiet Presence, the prayer throughout the day became more a sense of God's loving Presence.

As I live my days now, I am trying to get better at having prayer be a 24/7 reality. True prayer is mindfulness of God's Presence in each life moment. Following my breathing is a key way to pursue this constant prayer. I first met the breathing path in the Buddhist tradition. Following my breath, I find relaxation both for my body and also for sensing the Presence of God. Breathing techniques are numerous, and I find the variety helpful.

In recent time, I regularly include breathing in…through the image of God breathing into me….and breathing out…through the image of me breathing into God. And as I think of others in this 24/7 prayerfulness, I picture God's Presence in them and God's grace flowing through them, trusting God's companionship and Presence in their lives.

QUIET CENTER/HAPPY HEART/TRUSTING SPIRIT

Do not worry about anything,
but in everything by prayer and supplication
with thanksgiving let your request
be made known to God.
                                    Philippians 4:6

Sitting in my quiet chair, watching my wife head out to work, I asked myself, what is my deepest prayer for her as she goes into her days? I had 'retired' and her 'retirement' was two years off.

Out of that reflection, it came to me that I wanted for her to go about her days, her life, centered in deep quiet, carrying a happy, grateful heart and living her days with a trusting spirit. Since that time, I wish each one I meet a quiet center, a happy heart and a trusting spirit.

QUIET CENTER – Our minds take us all over the place with worries and preoccupations, fears and fantasies. Through the essence of spiritual practices of prayer, meditation and contemplation, we are invited to empty our minds into a deeper quiet. Centered then in that deep and empty quiet, we open ourselves to a stillness of seeing, to a calmness of hearing, in which we catch the wisdom, insight, love and peace of God that are before us and within us to receive and to live out. In this time, we don't just read the Bible and other books of wisdom. We go reflectively deeper into the greater Word and truth and meaning that call us into right paths of living and being. In this centeredness of deep, listening, seeing quiet, we are steadied to live the course of our lives through the busyness of our days. We are ready and open to follow the right unfolding of our lives. As Parker Palmer says: *"Before you tell your life what you intend to do with it, listen to what it intends to do with you."*

O rest beside the weary road, and hear the angels sing.

Hymn: It Came Upon A Midnight Clear

HAPPY HEART – One of the more common blessings includes these words…'go and enjoy.' With all the dimensions of this interesting human journey, from illness to death, from dangers to divisiveness, from fears to failures, I think God creates us to enjoy the gift of our days in our very human life. So as my wife heads off to work, I wish, that amidst her long to-do list, she will enjoy living her day. I debate whether I want to label this focus as happy heart or grateful heart, because gratitude is generally our best response to the gift of life. And as our gratitude increases, so does our joy, our happiness. One of our wisest practical and spiritual moves is to move from the pressures we face in living our days to the preciousness we continue to discover in the living of our days.For each day, each moment, each breath is a gift….to cherish, to enjoy, to live with gratitude.

Happy are those who make the Lord their trust.
Psalm 40:4

TRUSTING SPIRIT – As my wife goes off to work, I want her to carry as her core center, trust. Trust in God, yes. Trust in her efforts that she contributes to her day. Trust in the right unfolding of her life. What a difference it makes when our basic orientation is one of trust….in general and in God. In this trust orientation, we are more relaxed. We are more open to the good, life-giving flow that seeks to live in and through us. Trust.

Trust in the Lord forever,
for in the Lord God you have an everlasting rock.
Isaiah 26:4

QUIET TIME

The quieter you become, the more you can hear.

Ram Dass

In the deserts of the heart,
let the healing fountains start.

W .H. Auden

Growing up, I noticed devotional books on the side table of the particular chair that each of my parents would sit in alone in their separate rooms. Picking the books up occasionally, I noticed that these books were marked up, worn out and had writings in the margins and inside the covers. My parents referred to this 'quiet time' but never suggested to me that I should have a quiet time or read devotional books. I sensed that their 'quiet time' was also their prayer time.

Growing up with an awareness of 'quiet time,' when the Gospels spoke of Jesus going off to a quiet place to pray, that move to a quiet place became my favorite part of the life and way of Jesus.

In seminary, I became intrigued by the Desert Fathers and Mothers who escaped the chaos of life for the quiet of the desert. For them, like the Psalmists and my parents, in the 'quiet time' the great insights came and transformation began to happen. The more the 'quiet time' becomes a hunger, the easier it is to put down the to-do list and the ego needs. In the solitude that grows, I seek to simply be present in the moment, open to contemplate and think through what is before me and comes to me.

Dietrich Bonhoeffer wrote: *"For Christians the beginning of the day should not be burdened and oppressed with besting concerns for the day's work. At the threshold of the new day stands the Lord who made it."* And Fenelon wrote: *"Above all, try to save your mornings; defend them like a besieged city."*

The longer I live, the more I hunger for this quiet, for this solitude. In this quiet reflective time, my *"pilgrim soul"* hungers to be private and to go deep with myself, with God and with the issues that I face in life. And in this quiet, I pay more attention to my yearnings through which God nudges me and guides me.

I find that I am reading less and contemplating more on what I read and what I see and what I feel. As with the Desert Fathers and Mothers, this reflective quiet clarifies our issues and then demands that we head back into the world as a seeing, listening, loving presence. The role of deep quiet is awakening.

As the Prophet Isaiah puts it:

> *In returning and rest*
> *you shall be saved (led correctly, made well);*
> *in quietness and in trust shall be your strength.*
> *Isaiah. 30:15*

REALIGNING WITH GOD

....work out your own salvation
with fear/awe and trembling,
for it is God who is at work in you,
enabling you to will and to work
for God's good pleasure.
                              Philippians 2:12-13

Sin is a leading word in the church. This frustrates me. Focusing on sin seems to be an easy way to keep the people of the church in line, labeled, controlled, even threatened with punishment. The word sin is overused, too easily spoken as if pontificating about it will achieve the goal. The sin talkers talk at people in general while failing to make the Jesus move of 'come with me in a new way.'

The core root meaning of the word sin is to *miss the mark*. To me the obvious response to missing the mark is to realign with the mark. In worship the true confession of our sin is less a list of bad behaviors reported and more an honest confession of our awareness of wanting to realign ourselves with God through a faithful way of life and love. In my tradition, the confession of sin is followed by the declaration of forgiveness. And in God's heart that we know in Jesus Christ, there is forgiveness for us who miss the mark. In recent years, I have preferred to call this response to the confession of sin the Assurance of God's Love. This love is the energy, the engagement, the spirit that each of us needs in order to find new strength to re-align ourselves with God as we live our days.

I believe that the primary sermon that Jesus preached was on repentance. The gist of that sermon was Jesus' invitation to go with him in a different way, to live in a new way that would re-align us closer with God and God's life and love and being. Our human journey begins around our egos, begins with 'me.' Our journey with Jesus leads us to move from our ego to our soul, which is more about 'we' than 'me,' more about the larger life with God and others, beyond me.

This realignment with God and the way of Jesus is life-changing as we seek to move from centering on ourselves to realign with the Jesus way, with the heart of God. We realign, away from our old self and towards our new self.

These moves are new to us. We feel somewhat lost. We get to know ourselves in new ways. This call to a new way is honest about the challenges of living and being in a new way. In our trust in God and in the Jesus path, we find the courage and strength to pursue this transforming work of realignment. Realigned, we are selfless (you go first) and united (in this together).

God also has a role in this realigning. In most thinking minds, God is omniscient, all-knowing. The implication is that God is above all, beyond all and distant. Yet in the Christian understanding, this omniscient God chooses to move out of this beyond-us-distance to the within-us-nearness of engaging and companioning our very human way. Here the distant and vast One has the heart to choose to be present and close to the smallness of human life. In this move, God moves from omniscience that knows and holds all to faithful engagement that knows and holds us.

In this engagement, we simply give back to God who we are in all our fragility and fumbling. We are people called to change on our way to God, who does not change. In effect, we perish on the way to our new creation.

It is finally and completely in God's strength and Presence and love that we are realigned. And finally at home!

RIGHTEOUSNESS

*One is righteous because one responds
right and faithfully in each given relationship.*

The Hebrew word **Tzedakah** is translated as both righteousness and justice. I got to know the word best in Dietrich Bonhoeffer's Th.D. thesis. Bonhoeffer made clear that the use and lead meaning of the word in scripture was all about relationships. The deep Hebrew roots of the word focused on the concept of being '**right**' with the one before us, face to face, heart to heart, life to life. The 'righteousness of God' is God being for each of us, being right and just and fair with each of us. The 'righteousness of God' calls each of us to live out this righteousness…with God, with ourselves and with each other.

Bonhoeffer took me deep into the concept of being 'right' with the one before me as he stood up against the Nazi leadership during the Holocaust and was killed for seeking to stand rightly with his Jewish fellow citizens. My theology professor in seminary was a friend of Bonhoeffer during the 1930s in New York City, listening as Bonhoeffer wrestled with whether he should return to Germany and work for what was 'right.' At age 30, Albert Schweitzer gave up European fame in music, teaching and writing to do something 'right' for others in the middle of Africa. In India, Gandhi sought to be 'right' in the midst of the tensions of Hindus and Muslims and the tensions between the British and India over Indian independence. In El Salvador, Archbishop Oscar Romero found in the poor a Biblical call to be 'right' with and towards the poor and was killed for taking this stand.

As a child in the South, I grew up with signs at drinking fountains and on restroom doors that said "Whites only." I knew then that this was not 'right,' not being right with the one before me. In my lifetime, Martin Luther King, Jr. had the passion to press the issue of 'right,' of justice, of righteousness...and of course, was killed for it.

The point is not the killing. The point is how radical it is to move from caring about 'me' to caring about 'you'....as different as you may be from me. We humans hate change. We humans begin with 'me' and find it hard to move to 'you.'

Yet this Biblical word, righteousness, calls us to do our own Biblical growing up from feeling safe in our own differences to safely honoring others in their own differences.

To be 'right' with the one before us is a face to face honoring of the other and a safe space in which they can be freely who they are themselves. This concept has led me to quietly focus on people, looking and listening deeply into their spirit and being and life story and struggles, as part of my contemplation of how I want to be 'right' with them, to let them be safely themselves in my presence. Ethnic, racial, gender and class differences as well as the least among us and the poor before us demand the hard work of being right, righteous, just with the one before us. Even harder work may be in political and personality differences. Whether we like others or agree with them is not relevant in righteousness and justice.

This challenge of being 'right' with others starts with being 'right' with the very people with whom I spend the most time day by day. If we are going to walk the righteousness/justice path, we must lead with its dynamics in our families and closest friends and neighbors and work colleagues.

To this day I regularly hear the words righteousness and justice, yet much less often see those words lived out in their deepest meaning and passion.

RULES TO RELATIONSHIPS

He (Christ) has abolished the law with its
commandments and ordinances, that he might create in
himself one new humanity in place of the two, thus
making peace...

Ephesians 2: 15

At a public prayer vigil asking the State of Colorado for a pardon for a person questionably returned to prison, these thoughts were shared.

Jewish and Christian scriptures have a bunch of rules. In some faith communities, these rules are worshipped like gods. Our civil and democratic nation has a bunch of rules. In some places, these rules are worshipped like gods. Yes, for people of faith and the people of democracy, rules are very important and necessary to clarify values and to order our life together. Rules guide us on the human journey. Yet more than rules....there are relationships. The Hebrew prophets, including Jesus, strongly suggest that rules are simply coaching points for the greater value of honoring, redeeming and deepening relationships. And all these rules of faith point to two relationships: loving God and loving neighbor.

This tension between rules and relationships plays out in our nation all the time. With the penal system and the prison system on our minds, we find that rules have made us the most incarcerated nation in the world. And as we know, *the overuse of rules* and *over-sentencing* has led to 'the new Jim Crow' and today's racism that fills our prisons with persons of color.

On the way, the matter of relationships is too often thrown to the side of the road. Bureaucratic mistakes, limited government funding, and for-profit prisons on the whole choose rules over relationships. And of course, enforcing rules is easier, but not cheaper, than engaging in helping, healing, righting relationships.

Rules do need to be rightly enforced. Yet as we are finding with the help of DNA and with imperfect bureaucratic process, rules are not always rightly enforced. And sadly, in faith communities and in society, we too often fail to make the move that the prophets encourage: to move from rules to relationships; to move to honor, help, heal and caringly walk with others in relationship.

The move from rules to relationships involves moving from the written rule to the caring heart, moving to listen to and engage the life and renewal of the rule breaker.

When the prophet Micah invites us to 'do justice,' yes, rules help define what is just and right. Yet, justice is so much more than rules. Justice fulfills and completes itself in being faithful and caring to others....as Rene has lived out in concrete ways since his release.

When the prophet Micah invites us to 'love kindness,' we move from the rules to showing mercy in families and schools, to work places and neighbors, particularly for people in need of relationships that will help, heal and set right human life.

When the prophet Micah invites us to 'walk humbly' with God, the prophet begs that we not let the rules limit the depth of the great Relationship with God and others. Humility before God means humility before each other. Humility is the front door into building up the lives of others.

We pray that the power of the Governor and the Attorney General will have the humility and the caring sense of justice to listen beyond the rules to the relationship. May they move from 'just the rules….man…..just the rules' and from excessive mandatory sentences to the human person who seeks to live solidly and caringly in a new way.

SALT

You are the salt of the earth.
Matthew 5:13

I have learned through years of marriage that when my wife and I are out for a meal, I reach for the salt shaker and place it near her. More than I do, she loves the spirit and taste that salt adds to her food. Salt is one of the oldest and most ever-present food seasonings. Salt preserves food. Salt is essential for animal life. The tissues of animals contain larger quantities of salt than do plant tissues. Salt is a big player throughout the Bible for its role of seasoning and preserving, including adding salt to the animal and cereal offerings placed on the altar as sacrificial gifts to God.

In the Gospel of Mark, Jesus says: *"Have salt in yourselves, and be at peace with one another."(Mark 9: 50)* In other words, like salt, may you bring spirit and flavor to your own life and to the life of others, preserving life in others and in you. Be salt, Jesus asks, invites, commands us.

91

A friend volunteers at her son's elementary school. She is given one student or a small group who have special needs…from self-esteem to problematic habits to learning challenges. She has the time and energy to patiently help these students be more successful, more wholesome…as students….as persons. But mostly, she is a quiet, caring presence who seeks to bring out spirit and flavor in the lives of these students, seeking to preserve and build up in them a helpful and more confident sense of self. She is salt for the students.

Listening to patients in the hospital, I have learned that most often the best listeners and care givers to patients are not ministers and doctors and friends, but the cleaning ladies who listen and affirm…..and the nurses who quietly touch the forehead….and meaningfully ask: "how are you doing?" Salt.

To squat down to a child's eye level, look them in the eye, laugh with them…and say sincerely: *I believe in you…thanks for being you*….brings them alive…like salt.

I have long believed that the most important moment in the Sunday worship service is when the worshipers turn to each other at the end of the service. What do we bring to the person before us that brings them spirit and flavor, preserving and enhancing that person's life? Do they catch energy, interest and love from our quiet presence with them? Can they be loved in our listening to them and affirmed just as they are? Can we be that fully present [rather than distant], listening, sincerely interested, and happy to be with them, that we might be salt for them?

Being salt for each other, this face to face caring presence, deepens family life around the supper table [if the TV is turned off] and improves staff chemistry in corporate America. My best teachers had this salt quality of really caring, really being present with me. Think about how you are salt for others. Look less at what you do for them…including sharing your opinions….and look more at how your presence brings them alive, gives them a boost…salt…for being who they are. Being salt for others engages the other and changes us. To be salt is to go deep in living Jesus…in our lives.

SABBATH

You shall keep my Sabbaths, for this is a sign between
you and me throughout your generations,
given in order that you may know
that I, the Lord, sanctify you.
                                    Exodus 31:13

Jo and I found a cherished retreat center in upstate New
York called Chapel House. We went there for two or
three days occasionally for deep quiet, reading,
reflection, prayer, but mostly for a solitude that we
could not get in regular daily life. Years later, we find
this solitude in a mountain cabin, walking along an
ocean beach and in annual days in a Kansas monastery.
We are more and more interested in making each and
every day of our remaining lives a Chapel House day,
days of solitude, reflection, days that live out Sabbath.
Sabbath is going slow and deep with God. Sabbath
moments lead us to going slow and deep with others.

As I grow older and have more time to reflect on life, I notice that I get energy from solitude. This is certainly not as true for extroverts as for us introverts. Yet, the solitude that births new moments away from the fray and into the reflective holy is critical for all of us.

As the Gospels suggest, 'the Sabbath is made for humankind.' (Mark 2: 27) From the beginning, the concept of Sabbath wished for each of us the gifts of solitude and centeredness. Yes, the lead piece of Sabbath is our attention to God. But Sabbath is less a rule to obey and more a practice to grow to have open space in order to hang out with God more and more completely. God our source wants a great deal more of our attention than we give to God. In that spirit, God asks us to take a segment of our days to hang out more intentionally with God alone. This is the spirit of Sabbath. When I was growing up, some of our friends could not play cards or games or laugh or go out on Sundays. But Sabbath is so much more than this. In finding our various ways to do Sabbath, we push back on the human routine to make more space for God as our companion and completion.

In this spirit, we must daily learn how to rest...rest into God...rest into God's Presence. The role of this deeper quiet leads to awakening to God and awakening to the core joy and meaning of life.

Sabbath begins by taking every 7th day as rest with God as the major focus. To rest, to keep Sabbath is to honor God. Does it have to be just every 7th day? I don't think so. More important are the daily moments that are chosen to remember and honor God by backing off of our regular pace and going deeper in hanging out with God. We do Sabbaths, embracing weekly rests and other times of backing off, in order to make clear to ourselves that God is God and that we line up with God first and last. In Sabbath time, we wake up again to the Presence of God, whom we honor and acknowledge through this Sabbath move.

Wise ones believe that the final goal is a life lived completely with God as an ongoing and eternal Sabbath....in death, but also in our daily life. In the spirit of Francis of Assisi and other prayerful souls, we live our days as a seeing, listening, caring, loving presence, in and through God.

SHOW ME JESUS

...do everything in love...
I Corinthians 16: 14

To people who get in my face about Jesus, I want to say...show me Jesus...not with your words but with your spirit, your love, how you live your life. Yes, I know we are called to 'spread the Gospel,' and part of spreading the Gospel is testimony. Yet, my bias is that Jesus said little and loved much, and we should, also.

In my years of focusing on youth ministry, I loved to show a short film called "The Parable." The Jesus figure was a clown who walked through a county fair saying nothing. Some people harassed him unfairly. Some people he helped caringly. His silent presence was a living Jesus.

In the four Gospels, Jesus asks over 300 questions, ...then listens...seeking to engage with a listening, caring presence. Although we hear a lot about Jesus and much about what he said, in the Gospels he said less and engaged more as a listening presence.

Living Jesus is less talk and more loving engagement through walking the Way. The lead Christ figure in my life was my father. His key phrases were: 'you go first' and 'here, let me help you.' He listened more than he spoke, often saying little but asking questions and then being a fully listening presence. He was definitely an extrovert, but an extrovert who related relationally more than verbally. I was particularly touched by how caring he was to people who were socially 'the least' before him. Show me Jesus.

SILENCE

This is your hour, O Soul, your free flight into the
wordless.........silent, gazing, pondering.

Walt Whitman

When I made the high school football team as a
sophomore, my coach began to call me "Silent Cal."
He called out my silence because he picked up that I
loved silence. I was a class leader and bantered along
with the best of my teammates. But I did and do love
silence. With all due respect to my fellow classmates,
my favorite time in high school was quietly walking
alone to school through the woods. The mile walk was
through a forest of leaves and small animals and bird
songs. I filled up with silence each morning. That
silence carried me through the day.

Silence is both the path and the response to the
Presence of God with us. This silence is the lead place
and mode through which God speaks to us, nudges us,
guides us and leads us.

In God's deepest embrace, we are speechless before God, sharing a non-verbal relational presence together on the way to a mutual listening communion.

In the silence, God speaks and life's truths live. This sharing of silence with God reshapes how we walk with others. Out of this silence, we lead with listening, saying little out of that listening mode. To follow the Way, we are best at less talk and more engagement through listening and walking with others along the way.

Deep within this silence, I have less interest in seeking to tell the world the truth. I wish to move beyond talk to a seeing silence that becomes a neighbor who listens, cares, helps, loves, who lives out the truth. Everything that needs to be said can be expressed in how we live.

One day in a hospital, a doctor pulled me aside, asking if Gene Sweet was in my congregation. The doctor suggested that I talk with Gene, because Gene was not clear that he was about to die. That evening the thought came to me that I would go and visit this good friend and widower, saying nothing....silent.

The next morning I walked into Gene's hospital room. "Hi, Bill," he said. I nodded, pulled up a bedside chair and sat down. Out of the quiet, Gene spoke of the weather. I nodded. Gene spoke of his college, Purdue, losing in basketball the night before. I nodded.

After a bit more quiet, Gene said: "Well, I guess I am dying. It will be hard on my kids, but they will make it." I said, "Yes, you are. And I will really miss you, as your kids sure will. But your kids will make it through your death....with great love for you." I gave him a hug and said that I would see him in the morning.

Preach the Gospel at all times,
use words when necessary.

Francis of Assisi

SING TO GOD

Sing to God a new song.
Psalm 33:3

One of the ways we hang out with God is to sing to God. Most mornings of my life, driving to the gym or walking the beach, I sing to God, usually the Day Psalm (following) or verses from a church hymn.

The church teaches us that singing to God is a lead part of our worship, more formally our praise and adoration. In church the 'new song' is not so much about whether the music is centuries old. The new song is more to whom we sing. Do we sing about ourselves….the old song…or do we sing to God…the new song….the new direction of our song?

The psalms are a type of song: they are honest talks with God. Listen to the psalmist describe what it is like to hang out with God: *the Word is upright….the right path…upright posture…right-minded behavior.*

God is faithful, and God fills the world with "stick to us" love. God creates life, and in creation we see God first and best. Our emotion, gratitude and joy about this God are often best expressed in singing about this God and to this God.

Years ago I couldn't get a favorite tune out of my head. The song, "Try to Remember" comes from the off-Broadway show "The Fantasticks." Early one morning while watching our young kids, I took words from Psalm 118 and Psalm 100 and put them to that melody that I so love.

This is the day that the Lord has made.
Rejoice, be glad, give thanks, Alleluia.
God has made us, not we ourselves,
We are God's people, the sheep of the shepherd.
Enter the gates with thanksgiving,
The courts with praise,
Give God thanks and bless the Holy Name.
The Lord is good, the love is steadfast,
The faithfulness lasts to all generations.
This is the day that the Lord has made.
Alleluia. Alleluia. Alleluia. Alleluia.

SPEECHLESS AWE

The fear/awe of the Lord is the beginning of wisdom.
Proverbs 9: 10

As I read through the Bible, I keep meeting the phrase 'fear of the Lord.' The word fear has never worked for me. I wasn't catching a need to fear from the loving church people who clearly loved God and cared for me. It was clear from the people of faith around me that their spirit in relationship with God was love, respect, honor, in effect....awe. I soon realized that the better translation of the word fear is awe. Several hundred years ago, the word fear meant awe, but not today as it is commonly used. Also, the historic church sometimes seemed to choose 'fear' in order to control the people, 'sinners,' as they were so clearly labeled. When we choose control over the trusting dynamics of awe, we fail to go deep into the strength and help and grace that we find in God's love.

In awe of God, we are speechless in response to the vastness of God, the wonder of God's creation, the gift of life and God's love for us. It is clear that God, in the many ways of God, is with us. In God we find trust and strength and new energy from this Presence, this wonder, this life that we are given. And in this Presence, this God, we grow to trust that we can face ourselves and everything else in the world in God's strength and Presence and life. God IS with us.

Awe began to catch my attention as an elementary student in my summer time in the Colorado mountains. I would wander away from the rental cabin and sit on a rock or by the stream and watch and listen and be and see. Deer walking by. Fish swimming. Chipmunks checking me out. Birds in song and in search. In what I saw and heard and felt around me, those moments of beauty and wonder brought me more fully alive. Those moments of watching and listening filled me with more than what I saw. I grew a keener sense of the larger life beyond the animals, streams and trees, a deeper speechless awe. In creation and in those quiet larger moments, God was Present, that close, that engaged, with me.

Emerson loved to say that God is present with us in the nature around us, in the leaves, in the bird song, as "*the royal Presence*" of God in our days.

I still cherish the communion that I can get with creation, this creation that Richard Rohr calls the "first Bible." Yet, also through the years, as my interaction with humankind and the various seasons of life has increased, my sense of speechless awe has grown to include not only the outward creation, but also those green light moments in my days when right pieces come together for good and the needed insight or advice comes along.

In God the way is always there…the right way…awe. So over the past twenty years or so, I seek each day to watch how right pieces come together for good in God's World, leading again and again to the speechless awe of God's grace and guidance of our lives.

Yes, we humans must deal with our innate fears. Yet, the presence of speechless awe helps counter our fears and bend us toward faith, toward a greater trust.

I see this in people dying who trust God and in that trust let go into death, with a glow, with a trust, falling into a deeper life with God. In recent time, as I identify my fears, I am more comfortable to face what unfolds, because in God I will have the strength and the faith to face what I must face.

'The awe of the Lord.'

STOP, LOOK AND LISTEN

...to do justice, and to love kindness,
and to walk humbly with your God.
Micah 6: 8

My first few years, I lived in a 700 person town outside of Dallas. When we drove somewhere, I would sit in the back seat by the right window of the late 1940s green Plymouth Suburban station wagon. One vacant lot south of our home was a railroad track. When we stopped for a train, I would look out at the white crossing sign, so simple, so worn, giving its warning: Stop...Look...Listen.

Stop...Look...Listen. Even as a child, I felt something mystical, something catching about those three words. It was more than "look out for a train coming." It was a nudge on how to be, on how to live one's life. Throughout my life, every "Stop...Look...Listen" sign catches my attention, far beyond watching out for a train. It invites me to clarify my proper place in the larger whole of life.

When my application to Dartmouth College asked for a philosophy of life in twenty-five words or less, I knew right away what I would write: Stop for others, look for good, listen for God.

Stop for others: The Benedictines advocate greeting Christ in the person before you. In that spirit, we take the human life before us seriously, with a seeing, listening, loving presence. Stopping for others is saying little but listening more. Stopping for others is seeing them more clearly, loving them more dearly and walking with them more nearly…day by day.

Look for good: Media makes money by focusing on stories that will sell. Most often that is the bad news. If we are going to find the good side of the human story, we must do the reporting ourselves. The good is there, in each person, in each event, in each challenge.

Listen for God: My primary devotional book calls me to pay attention to the "promptings within." The Psalms affirm:

"God will be our guide forever." Ps 48:14

WAITING FOR AND WITH GOD

Our soul waits for the Lord;
God is our help and shield.
Our heart is glad in God,
Because we trust in God.
                          Psalm 33: 20-21

Henri Nouwen was a huge coach for me. Over a twenty year period, I read nearly every book he wrote. My favorite line of his is that 'we wait for God and we wait with God.'

Nouwen wrote this out of the context of the story of Mary and Elizabeth waiting for God's promises and help and blessings in their pregnancies. Waiting for God and the moves of God is the lead mind set throughout the Bible for people of faith. But what took me deeper, and with joy, was Nouwen pointing out that we don't just wait for God. In God, we live our lives waiting <u>with</u> God who waits with us through the events and days of our lives. Waiting with God suggests a deeper Presence and truth in our relationship with God. Waiting with God, we have a place by God's side and God has a place by our side.

The fellowship of waiting together is the nature of our relationship in and through and with God. Waiting with God is affirming that we are in this together, present with each other, at-one with each other. We wait for God. We wait with God. In this the Psalmist experiences *"making my steps secure…a new song in my mouth…trust."(Psalm 40:2-3)*

To wait <u>for</u> God, we wait for the help and the love-strength that we find in God as God goes through life with us. We wait for God to lead us in the 'right' paths. *(Psalm 23:3)* We wait for God's strength as we walk the paths that we are given to walk.

To wait <u>with</u> God is to hang out with God, who all along is present with us. The Presence of God clarifies the right balance for our lives. Psalm 32:8 suggests what this waiting with God does: *"I will instruct you and teach you the way you should go. I will counsel you with my eye upon you."* Waiting with God is the core of prayer…hanging out with God in each breath and moment and thought…a life of prayer. In that spirit, Psalm 33:7 puts it: *"you are a hiding place for me."* Here we find a quiet place to be just us together.

114

We wait together. We let go of the world for a bit, and to grow closer to each other and go deeper together before we then return to daily life in the world, together.

The Desert Fathers and Mothers escaped to the desert of North Africa to flee the Roman culture and to hang out with God….waiting together, living together as God and human together. But a couple of funny things happened as they waited with God in the desert. First, without their preoccupation with the human world to distract them, they had more time to notice their own individual fears and obsessions as well as their personality quirks. This drove them crazy. They needed God's Presence to give them courage and strength to accept and to be the human persons they were. Secondly, the more deeply and fully they waited with God, the more they found that God's loving Presence moved them to go back into the interesting human world to share this love. They returned with God, waiting with God, as they loved their neighbors with a seeing, listening, loving, waiting presence.

In the story of God parting the waters in the Exodus, a path appears that was not seen before. And the people do nothing but keep still, continuing to wait for and with God. Not to keep still in the midst of difficult times risks failing to see the 'saving'/ 'deliverance' way that may be right there before us. To wait for and with God opens us to the help of the flow of God's grace before us. Faith trusts in this helping companionship. As the hymn puts it:

> *Be still my soul, the Lord is on your side;*
> *Bear patiently the cross of grief or pain;*
> *Leave to your God to order and provide;*
> *In every change God faithful will remain.*
> *Be still, my soul; your best, your heavenly Friend;*
> *Through thorny ways leads to a joyful end.*
>
> *Hymn: Be Still My Soul*

WORD OF GOD

Your word is a lamp to my feet
and a light to my path.
                                Psalm 119:105

Through my years of greeting folks following worship, some people tell me how much they appreciated what I said about this or that. Often I did not say exactly what they had heard. These moments remind me that what God says to each of us is so much more than the words in the sermon, so much deeper than an exact scripture verse. The Word of God is first and last what gets through to us, nudges us and shapes us beyond the specific words spoken and read. This Word is less a literal word heard and more a deeper word sensed and known through insights and truths that show up within us. Yes, this Word received within us is the revealing work of God's Spirit, planting within us a deeper truth and guidance. We receive, engage and grow into this Word, even though this Word is finally more than we can completely understand or thoroughly see...simply a light on the Way.

There are important things that we can do to be open to God's Word to us. We can remember that although the Bible has lots of rules, these rules simply coach our relationship with God and coach our relationship with others. We can read the Bible with a listening openness, writing our questions and insights in the margins, and letting the verses themselves and the teachings of others take us deeper into God's living, dynamic Word in us. We can join with the Psalmist in asking God to *"teach me wisdom in my secret heart."* (Ps. 51: 6)

Scripture meets us as hints of truth, as poetry points. The Bible is open and free for God's Spirit to speak and guide and shape us. On the Way, the organized ideas of our faith teachings and worship liturgies are road maps to a deeper sense of God's Word to each of us.

We can also quiet down into listening moments of empty silence. Or as Benedict wrote: *"Listen with the ear of your heart."* As the silence stills our minds, a space is created in which to receive, to catch, to hear a larger Word to us.

Questions (ours and God's) are critical aids that help open us up to God's Word to us. In this spirit, Jesus asked over 300 questions in the Gospels. This Jesus, who is so often quoted, did more asking and listening than teaching and preaching. Questions open us up to go deeper into the truth before us and within us.

The Word of God is God's Word to us. This living Word of God is so much more than we can handle, grasp or even get perfectly clear or right. Our searching for clarity is stymied by the mystery of all that God is. And our understanding is limited by the limits of our own thinking, speaking and insights. We treat it, speak it, live it humbly, because it is so much more than us. This living Word of God is always after us, whether through a sermon or a reading of scripture or devotional books or a phrase by a friend or an insight that sneaks up on us in a passing moment. This Word sneaks up on us, getting into us and shaping us in ways that we can never really pin down or possess. Our openness to it moves beyond a need for exactness and proof to a sensing trust that God's Word will show up within us and faithfully lead us. We simply catch the nudges until this Word has caught us.

Yet, we never completely have it. We never completely possess or control this Word before us and within us. This gap between God's Word to us and our grasp of that Word is not to be filled, but to be honored by our trusting faith. In this gap, we are simply held by this love that this Word is. As the saints so often say…'we know God…but not much else for sure.' God and God's Word are finally more than we can grasp or completely handle. We simply seek to live into this Word and this Truth, enjoying our smallness before God's largeness.

EPILOGUE

MY ROSARY

At 30,000 feet, I sat next to a church member who grew up in the Catholic tradition but joined our Presbyterian congregation when she married one of our members. We were flying home with a church group from a medical mission trip to El Salvador.

I asked her: Do you still do your Rosary (Catholic prayer)? She flinched at first, wondering about the right thing to say to the minister. But thankfully, she sighed and chuckled, saying with confidence, "Yes, I do. I try to do my Rosary daily."

I said back to her: I do enough morning prayers that I think I will make them become my Rosary. I had been doing several prayers in my mind for years, but in that moment it came to me that I would embrace this personal practice as my own Rosary. My Rosary of twenty years follows.

And your Rosary?

†

The Day Psalm

This is the day that the Lord has made.
Rejoice, be glad, give thanks, Alleluia.
God has made us, not we ourselves,
We are God's people, the sheep of the shepherd.
Enter the gates with thanksgiving,
The courts with praise,
Give God thanks and bless the Holy Name.
The Lord is good, the love is steadfast,
The faithfulness lasts to all generations.
This is the day that the Lord has made.
Alleluia. Alleluia. Alleluia. Alleluia.

From Psalms 118 and 100;
tune: "Try to Remember"
from the off Broadway show "The Fantasticks"

†
"i thank you God for most this amazing day:
for the leaping, greenly spirits of trees
and a blue true dream of sky;
and for everything which is natural
which is infinite which is yes"
E.E. Cummings

†

Look to this day, for it is life, the very life of life.
And in its course lay all the varieties and realities
of your own existence.
The bliss of growth, the glory of action,
the splendor of beauty...
For yesterday is already a dream
and tomorrow is only a vision.
But today well lived
makes every yesterday a dream of happiness
And every tomorrow a vision of hope.
Such is the salutation of the dawn.
                                              Sanskrit

†

Bless O Lord this day to our use and us to your service.
Guide us in the ways of truth
and make us ever mindful of the needs of others.

†

Lord Jesus, be our holy guest,
our morning joy, our evening rest.
And with this gift of day, impart
your peace and love to every heart.

†

Almighty God, unto whom all hearts are open
and no secrets are hid.
Cleanse the thoughts of our hearts
by the inspiration of your Holy Spirit,
that we may completely love you
and worthily make you large.
                                        Episcopal prayer

†

"El Senor es me pastor. Nada me falta."
(...The Lord is my pastor/shepherd. I lack nothing...)
God leads me to lie down in green pastures,
To rest by still waters.
God restores my soul, my life.
God leads me in the right paths.
Even though I live through dark and hard times,
I will not be afraid.
For God is with me like a shepherd's rod and staff.
God's grace prepares a table before me
In the presence of rough events and persons,
My head is anointed with oil.
My cup of blessing overflows.
Surely goodness and mercy shall pursue me
All the days of my life.
I will live in and with God
In these days and forever.
Psalm 23

†

The Lord's Prayer

Our Father/Mother, who is with us now as in heaven,
Holy is your name and being.
Your world be our world, your way be our way,
On earth as it is in heaven.
Give us this day your daily gifts.
And forgive us as we forgive others.
Keep us in your strength in times of testing
And deliver us from evil.
For you are the kingdom and the power and the glory.
In each breath, each step, forever.
Amen

AFTERWORD

COMPANIONS ON THE WAY

*I lift up the names of some of the many people
who walked with me, mentored me, loved me:*

*My family, especially Jo, Mark, Molly,
my dad and my mom*

*Faith leaders, especially Rev. Walter Dickson,
Rev. David Yohn, Rev. E.O. Kennedy, Rev. Bill Bell,
Rev. Jim Gordon, Rabbi Steve Foster, Rev. Paul Martin*

*Teaching mentors, especially Paul Lehmann,
Walter Wink, Sid Skirvin, Morton Kelsey,
Sister Mary Dingman, Roy Oswald*

*Authors, especially Agnes Sanford, Jack Sanford,
Karl Barth, Albert Schweitzer, Dietrich Bonhoeffer,
Nikos Kazantzakis, Henri Nouwen, Thomas Merton,
George Buttrick, Walter Brueggemann,
Frederick Buechner, Bill Coffin, Richard Rohr,
Eugene Peterson, Parker Palmer,
Eric Law, Robert Johnson*

YOUR MARGIN NOTES